IMPRESSIVE CUSTOMER SERVICE

at its greatest…

Trishuna Brown

ISBN: 10: 0-578-40313-7
ISBN-13: **978-0-578-40313-7**

CONTENTS

ACKNOWLEDGMENTS

I thank the Lord for the knowledge that he has given me to share with people whom I meet daily. I am forever grateful to my husband Chadrick for all of his support, patience and love. I thank my three girls, Cobi, Cameron, and Calah, for always believing in my projects and being my helping hands. I give kudos and thanks to my team at work for teaching me as I teach them. You are a great team! Last but not least, I thank my mom, Rosa Lee Bentley for teaching me and modeling for me what it means to care for others and to help meet their needs. I learned a remarkable lesson in selflessness from you mom. I could not have written this book if I had not witnessed your struggles and your determination to persevere. I thank you and love you with all of my heart.

PREFACE

It has been about a year now and I know in my heart that I am supposed to write this book; however, with school, work, family and several other things, I just could not reach that frame of mind I needed to pull it together. I thought about the title after title but none of them seemed right, so I put the writing aside. Then, one day the title came. I watched a movie in which the main character was seeking an answer to a problem. The answer was right under his nose, but he did not notice it until the end of the movie. Suddenly, he realized that the answer was in his house. Ah ha!!!! I too realized that the answers I needed to complete this book have been right under my nose the entire time. I also recognized that often times we are too close to the answer that we are seeking, and we miss it; therefore, we have to step back and look at the picture from a different perspective.

I am a very friendly person and I try to be kind to people that I encounter. My daughter took her car to be serviced. Because I like to be the first in line, we arrived at the auto service store bright and early. As we waited in the lobby area, I noticed another young lady who was also waiting. Being the talkative person that I am, I walked over and started a conversation. As we were talking, I noticed that her blouse was inside out. I recognized that her blouse needed to be corrected. Although, I am a very friendly, talkative person, I found it very difficult to tell her that her blouse was inside out. Well, my customer service skills kicked in and I said in a very low and I mean very low voice (because I talk loud most of the time), "Your blouse is inside out." She looked down, smiled and thanked me for telling her. She told me that she had to get dressed in the dark so that she would not wake up the grandchildren so early. After I stepped away, a young man walked over and whispered the same statement to her. We all had a ball laughing about it. After the roar of laughter ended, she said, "I wonder who else would care to tell me that I was dressed out of order." It was then that the title of this book came to mind: At Its Greatest, Impressive Customer Service.

I love serving and helping others. I am passionate about it. One thing that I learned early on is that your gifts and calling follow you. We cared enough about our neighbor that we did not want her to look odd. Excellent customer service is a must as we serve other people. If this is your gift or calling, perform it with excellence and passion. This is what I am going to talk about in this book. As you read, I hope that its content will help bring out your greatest customer service skills.

1 THE TEACHING

Before now, I never thought of writing a book on such a valuable subject as customer service. I began hearing from others that my customer service skills are contagious and positively affect people that I serve daily. I asked myself, "Why do I have great people skills?" I believe that it is something that I was born with, that I was taught and that someone modeled for me. As you read on, you will see that it is a combination of all three. It is part of my gifting and calling. I cannot run from it if I tried. As I told you earlier, I automatically engaged when I spoke to the young lady about her blouse.

As a little girl, I remember watching my mother make people laugh when they were feeling down. She was always a happy woman. I can't recall very many times that I saw my mother sad. We did not have a very big house, but I can recall walking out of my bedroom and stumbling over a log of a person that she took in because he had nowhere to go. (Now, this would not be the safest thing to do today. I'm not saying take folks in, so be careful with that). This was the first of many lessons I would learn about serving others. I can't begin to tell you the number of people she fed in our neighborhood. She was a woman of service. Not only did she serve people in her community, but she also served people at her job.

At an early age, I was her assistant at work. I can remember it as though it was yesterday. We were up around five o'clock a.m., walked about two miles to the bus stop, and waited on the bus in the heat, cold, and rain. The bus ride to the hotel where she worked was a long ride. This was fun for me because I liked to sit by the window and imagine I was on a theme park ride so I really wasn't concerned about the details of the journey to her workplace. My mother took so much pride in her job as she made beds and cleaned the rooms. The guests loved her. They would talk and laugh joyfully with her. This was a hotel where the guests returned each year, so they knew her and the excellent customer service that she rendered. She was the best housekeeper at this hotel of twenty-five to thirty rooms. Her boss always complimented her on her extraordinary work and gave her bonuses as well. If she was upset about anything, she never showed it at her workplace. She always encouraged the guests and focused her attention on them and other people that she served. Wow! What an awesome display of selfless service. My mother walked to the bus stop every day and did not complain or allow the walk to affect her ability to serve others well. Nowadays, a walk to the bus stop for some people will upset them so greatly that the one little walk (short or long) will cause a barrage of complaints and send their customer service skills out of the window. As I said earlier, not only was I born with the gifting of excellent customer service, but I was also taught how to serve, and it was modeled for me by my mother. That being said, my desire is to teach others how to serve well and to model excellent customer service for them.

I used the word selfless to describe how my mother served others. This seven-letter word is so important to serving others. Impressive service is not about us. I want you to think about something. There are days when you might wake up feeling good and you discover that your spouse forgot to replace the tissue in the bathroom. Your response is, "For the life of me, I can't get this man/woman to replace the tissue roll." Steaming mad, your "good morning" feeling is gone. The result is that everyone who crosses your path feels the backlash of the tissue episode. We allow simple things to negatively affect our ability to serve others well. For example, at one point or another in our work history, we have all encountered people whose faces are balled up as if they had just eaten a sour lemon (especially early in the morning). There have also been times when we displayed the sour lemon face. But you, being the concerned person, you are, recognize the face and you automatically shift into encouragement mode. Your first question: "What is wrong?" You receive an answer—a long one at that. You hear about the long bus ride, the little old lady who talked continuously and just couldn't be quiet, and the person who forgot the deodorant. Finally, you are being the concerned and selfless person that you are, ask yourself, "Why did I ask that question?" Allow me to answer it for you. It is simple: because you cared enough to ask. Sometimes people are unable to part with their personal problems, so they bring them to work. While this is not a good practice, it happens. Their focus on their problems affects their service. The result is that the customer unknowingly receives the impact of the problem. When this occurs, remember that you have the power to determine how you will respond or react. A positive response makes all the difference when interacting with people. Key point: No one or nothing should be able to ruin your ability to provide impressive and excellent customer service. Remember that excellent customer service is not about us, but it is about your team and the customers that you serve. We can make each day a great day!

While I had a great mentor in my mother, I encourage you to find that person who can help you to polish your customer service skills. Look for those people in your organization who possess excellent service skills and habits, choose one person and ask him or her to mentor you. I believe that the person who has a positive attitude, who gets the job done, who works well with others and who tackles challenges as if they were opportunities is the person who is the ideal mentor.

Let's Work on It

 In the table below, write the names of three people who you believe would be a great mentor to you. List the different attributes they possess. After you have listed all three (or maybe you have only two), narrow them down and choose a mentor who you think will be honest with you about the areas in which you need improvement and who will teach you well.

Name	Attributes	Why a potential mentor?
Example: Mary Lee	*Critical thinker*	*Can teach me to think critically and positively.*

Remember, identify at least three people who are potential mentors so that you have a substitute in the event that your selected person is not available.

Let's Work on It

Exceptional customer service doesn't magically appear; it is developed and refined over time. So, let's work on developing our skills. Begin with self. What do we want people to hear, see, and feel when we serve them? If we want their experience to be positive, then we should give thought to how we will speak and act. Specifically, our behavior says a lot about us. Our body language, facial expressions, and eyes speak volumes (and loudly) before we utter a word. People hear the unspoken statements, see the actions (welcome or unwelcome) and feel uncertain or confident about the level of service that might be given. Think about this. Have you ever walked into an organization and you were received with that "what" look? The look that asks the question, "What do you want?" How did that look make *you* feel? Would you want your customer to feel awkward or uncomfortable because of your "unspoken" language?

Sometimes our words and the manner in which we express them can make our customers feel badly. Imagine this scenario: It is 8:00 a.m., you need assistance with finding a particular office; you are met with, "Can I help you?" Depending upon the way the statement is delivered, you, the receiver just might respond with a simple, "No thank you."

Whatever happened to, "Good morning, how may I help you today?" Which response would you prefer? Customers are important to every business and organization and it is incumbent upon us who serve them to provide them with exceptional service. Remember, you have the ability to create a positive encounter for the customer through your actions and words.

I have worked in customer service for many years and it is sad to hear a customer say, "I wish you could teach XXX Business how to give the service that you guys give." Why should anyone walk away from a business feeling unwelcomed? This should not be but it happens. Poor customer service can reflect poorly upon the brand of any company. As customer service providers, we are charged with making our customers feel welcome and appreciated. As you read further, you will learn to provide exceptional service so that no customer will walk away wishing he or she had *not* encountered you.

I believe that exceptional customer service is required in every organization and should be a characteristic of the organization's culture. One way that a culture of excellent service is created is through training and modeling. Ongoing training ensures that employees know how to greet and converse with customers as well as how to handle customers' frustrations. Further, continued instruction keeps us abreast of trends in how to provide the best service at all times. Modeling impressive customer service helps others to improve their skills. If you are a member of a customer service team, watching others can help you to be on your best game at all times. In fact, modeling can be contagious. Try it!!!

Excellent customer service should not be limited to customer service representatives, but it should be practiced and modeled at every level of the organization or company (executives, managers, supervisors, leaders, etc.). I have observed a number of customer service reps who became so frustrated with how managers responded to them and treated them that they quit their jobs. It was difficult for them to separate the job and the frustration. In other words, they blamed the job for the frustration rather than the manager who was the root cause. There are times when team members are treated unfairly by managers because the manager has poor customer service skills. If the manager has poor customer service skills, the staff is likely to mimic the same behavior. This is what I call the blind following the blind and at this point, the whole business falls into the ditch. I remember driving up to a drive-through window and the clerk was so rude. I asked to speak to the manager about the poor service since I was paying my money for the product. The manager was equally as rude. My first thought was, "I will never come back to this place again." No manager should want that kind of service for his or her company or organization nor should the team members be shorted because the manager failed to provide the necessary training to improve their skills. Great customer service is in all of us, but we have to learn how to develop, refine, and model our skills.

Now, you reader, is a wonderful person because you are a person of service. To be a person of service, you have to know you. To know you requires that you love you and display a selfless character. These two actions will set the standard for impressive customer service. Which one do you prefer: I like me, or I love me? The one that you choose is the one you use for yourself and others. The selfless person is able to exhibit self-control under pressure. He or she knows how to walk away when he feels as if he has been mistreated or during a heated conversation. This person also knows how to limit his or her words (they don't have to have the last word.). I recall working in a hair salon and one customer was so rude. I found myself trying to have the last word and the battle of words went on and on until I got tired. I finally shut up so that she would hush. She didn't hush; she just fussed her way out of the door. I knew then that I did not ever want to go through a similar encounter again. No one wins in a fuss box match. Someone has to step outside the ring. I learned a couple of things that day. It is not the baddest one who hits my hand; it is the baddest one who walks away from my hand. I understood clearly that day that I have the authority to turn a heated situation into a calm situation through humility and understanding. So, I share this with you. Take charge, model humility and understanding!!!

Let's Work on It!

Are you ready to greet the next customer who enters your office or business? What posture are you displaying? Are you leaning on the wall talking to other team members or are you slightly swinging in your chair talking on the phone? Frankly, I don't recommend either of the above if your ultimate goal is to model exceptional customer service. It is not good to have sidebar conversations when customers are in your office. These conversations can make your customer feel uncomfortable and unwelcome. Loud conversations and laughter can also create negative impressions and portray your work environment as a playground.
Sit with your feet flat on the floor. Make sure your mind is alert as you wait to greet the next customer.

Write below two positive positions (sitting and standing) that show your customers you are ready and prepared to serve them as they walk into the office.

Sitting	Standing

2 SET YOUR MIND

How do you start your day? Is your mind full of thoughts from yesterday's events, concerns and issues or is your mind refreshed, focused and excited about a new day?

Think about it. There are some people who wake up thinking about what happened yesterday. They allow yesterday to be their today and their minds are consumed with all of yesterday's issues. Know this, today is a brand-new day. New events will take place and new people will show up to be served. If your mind, customer service rep, is consumed with negativity and past events, then your focus will not be sharp. So, forget about the interaction with the disgruntled customer on yesterday. You have a new customer today. Serve this customer with enthusiasm. Don't think about the manager who chose not to speak yesterday, you initiate the greeting today. Set your mind. It is a brand-new day. The focus is not on you and how you feel but your focus is to make sure that your customers are served well. Choose the mindset and perspective that you want to start your day. Remember that the choice you make, positive or negative, will follow you all day. Think about it!!!

Now, I have asked you to set your mind; however, know that every customer will not have pushed the button to set his or her mind at the beginning of the day. Some are going to be rude regardless. You can try with all your might to provide the best customer service on the planet, but the rudeness will prevail. I believe that when a customer is rude or upset, there is a reason behind the behavior. I am not one to make excuses for rude behavior, but I believe that some people may not always be aware of their behavior. "How so?" you ask. Based on my own experiences, people can be so engrossed in their own problems that they do not hear themselves as they speak to others and whatever they have experienced before the encounter with you contributes to their response. They unleash their hurt, anger, and disappointment upon the first person they encounter...you. You have set your mind for the day and you are determined to stop the rude behavior. In this instance, you focus on how to positively engage the angry customer so that the rude behavior does not continue. Now this tactic might not work in every situation because some people just choose to be rude regardless. However, a calm, soft voice and positive body language can diffuse some situations. Employing understanding and offering to find a solution to the problem works well.

I highly recommend setting your mind at the beginning of your day. You never know what you will encounter during the day; therefore, it is best to be prepared.

Up to now, I have focused on external customers, but I want to remind you that internal customers experience similar issues also. The positive mindset and the steps I mentioned earlier work internally as well. I recall a young lady who I would often see at work. I learned that she worked in another department. She would never speak, and she would barely raise her head to look at herself in the bathroom mirror. It was not my business to know why she behaved as such, but it was my business to make sure she had a great day. She was my internal customer. I finally approached her. I learned her name, job title, and work location. One question ended in a continuous and delightful conversation. Had I not engaged her in a conversation, she probably would have remained quiet and aloof.

Just a thought: I wonder how effective was her customer service prior to our encounter? I am not bragging on myself but how we approach others, positively or negatively, can have an impact on others' behavior. Hopefully, I impressed her enough to make her want to positively engage her customers. Each time I meet this young lady now, there is always laughter and positive conversation. I believe that engaging people in wholesome conversations and laughter create a positive atmosphere. This kind of atmosphere is needed in setting the stage for excellent customer service. Be powerful and positive in your thinking. You can make a difference in the customer's experience. Your mindset should always be focused on exceptional. Don't help a customer because it is just your job, help the customer because you love your job and your desire is that the customer has an exceptional experience. Answer the phone because you are excited about assisting the caller with his or her concerns not just because there is no one else to answer the phone. Go the extra mile. Do everything you can to serve well.

Set your mind on exceptional.

Let's Work on It

Think about ways to start your day well. I suggest practicing affirmations, calming techniques, and meditation. List three of these below and practice at the start, the middle and the end of your day. Your practice will eventually become a habit.

Start of day	Middle of day	End of day

3 DRESS FOR SUCCESS

At the start of your day, I want you to know that it is going to be a great day! The most important word in the previous sentence is "you". The word *you* are important because you have the power to command the events of your day. Think about how you feel when you arise. Do you feel like a skirt girl or a suit boy or do you feel like a pants girl or a necktie boy? The way you dress has a lot to do with how you feel. If you just rolled out of bed, it is likely that you will dress like you just rolled out of bed. Furthermore, if you *feel* like you just rolled out of bed, then it is possible that your productivity will suffer.

Imagine this scenario. You have styled your hair perfectly. Not one strand is out of place. You selected a suit and accessories that exude professionalism and confidence. As you look in the mirror for the last inspection before you leave for work, you feel absolutely confident that you are going to have a great day. The first person that you encounter compliments you on how nice you look.

That one compliment can steer you in the direction of a positive and assured mindset.

It has been my experience that some people take you more seriously when you look professional and act professionally. One word of advice, don't just throw on clothes, get dressed for your exceptional day! I recall working for a company where the Human Resources staff always dressed professionally. There was something different about how they walked--they walked with confidence; how they talked—they talked with confidence; and how they collaborated professionally with others. Even though I was a Clerk, I knew with certainty that I wanted to have that same sense of professionalism in my dress, my conversations and in my walk. As I reflected on what I observed, I made a deliberate decision to dress for success because I wanted to make a difference in the same way that the HR team had made a difference.

I could have thought of every excuse in the world to support why I did not dress professionally; however, I absolutely refused to do so. I immediately drove to the thrift store. I walked in and found nothing. I really wasn't focused. It just so happened that one of my co-workers was an expert thrift-store shopper and she taught me the strategies of becoming an astute thrift-store shopper. She schooled me on which days to go to the thrift store and how to find spectacular deals. I followed her instructions and found the best career focused clothes for work. In my pursuit to change my image (attitude and dress), I encouraged others to do the same. I now looked like the professional my organization needed me to be. I noticed that customers approached me differently and I responded to them differently all because I chose to not settle for the normal day. I chose to have an exceptional day.

My mother once told me the story that she owned two dresses (yes, just two) to wear to school. She explained that she washed and folded her dresses like they cost a million bucks. She would put on her dress and walk to school with her head high and books and pencils in hand ready to learn. I will never forget the profound advice that she gave me. She said, "It is not about how much you have but what you do with what you have." To this day, I take pride in the way I represent the organization for which I work. It is imperative that you represent yourself and your company well. Be driven to dress for success.

Let's Work on It

So, you ask, "How do I dress for success?" I'm glad you asked. First, remember that you are not following the path of rolling-out-of-bed attire, but you are aiming to dress for success. Therefore, you will need to create the professional look you desire. Secondly, think about the clothes, accessories and shoes that will achieve the look that you have created. Finally, plan a layout of your outfits for the week and follow it. Not only will you feel great about how you look, but you will also perform well.

Now, let's plan the wardrobe for the week following the steps above.

Tops	Bottoms	Accessories	Shoes

Note: Think about the colors you choose. Bright colors create a cheerful mood and natural colors create a calm mood.

4 THE COMPANY YOU KEEP

Outward appearance is everything, but we also have to be careful of the company we keep…the people with whom we associate. Think about the people who are your acquaintances at work. Are you among the group who hangs around the water cooler casting stones and bashing others or are you watchful of what you think and say about others? You hold the key to prevent this kind of behavior from becoming a part of your workspace. If you are constantly around people who participate in gossiping, criticizing, and tearing others down, I suggest that you find a different group of people whose conversations and attitudes are focused and positive. Just as you are gossiping and belittling others, there will come a time when people (maybe those same water-cooler friends) will do the same to you.

This toxic behavior spreads quickly and can negatively affect an organization. Specifically, when the morale in an organization is already diminished, toxic conversations about people and the organization can push the morale into a deeper slump. My question to you, "Are you a problem starter or a problem solver?"

Another popular "water cooler" conversation is money. Yes, I agree that money is important, but I urge you, don't allow money to be the primary reason why you do your job. Perform your job with a spirit of excellence because there is a community waiting to be served. Again, toxic conversations, half-truths, and negative attitudes can shed a bad light on you and others. Remember that people listen, watch and judge based on what they hear and see.

A former manager once told me, "Trishuna, when you finish your day at work and turn off that light switch, make sure you have done all you could do to make sure things were done right because you have to own it." What awesome advice. Own it. Now I'm going to ask you the same thing. Remove my name and place your name in that space. At the end of your workday, how do you feel? Have you given it your all or have you spent more time than necessary at the water cooler with people who might not have been the best group to spend time with; or do you see your day as "a mess" or productive? Now is the time for you to reflect and think about how effective you are with your team and in your organization. Develop a positive mindset about your team and your organization. Set goals that will help the team grow and meet the needs of the internal and external customers you serve. The customers are a remarkable asset to every organization. Further, it is imperative that you meet their needs with excellence and simplicity. I employ you to make an informed decision to elevate your customer service skills to the level of excellence. I promise that you will not regret it. Become the best!

Let's Work on It

List the aspects of your job that you really enjoy then list the aspects of your job that you would like to change. I believe that your *like* list will be greater than your *change* list. When you complete each list, find ways in which you can integrate the changes into your department and then discuss your ideas with the team.

Likes	Changes

A change will never occur unless you begin.

5 SELFISHNESS

During my career, I have learned that serving is not about self. Service is about others; therefore, selflessness is required. The definition of selfless is having no concern for self; unselfish.[1] The selfless person is concerned about meeting the needs of and helping to provide the wants of others. To be a person of excellence in customer service, your focus is not on you but on the customers, you serve; therefore, your personal concerns should not be at the forefront of your mind. Remember the rude person I spoke about earlier, my reaction and how that situation worked itself out? When you are able to counter rudeness with kindness and understanding, the person will (in most cases) calm down. Again, we never know what people are experiencing so if we focus on meeting the needs of the customer, it is very likely that there will be a favorable outcome for all concerned. I encourage you to allow selflessness to be second nature in all that you do.

There was a customer who made a purchase in my department, but she lost the product. It was critical that she replace this product. The problem was that she did not have enough money to purchase it again. One of the team members asked me to explain the process to her. As I explained the process, she became very emotional and pleaded for help. I understood her need and suddenly I was moved to pay for the product for her. This is something I don't always do but I understood the urgency of her situation. One of the new team members who observed the interaction stated, "You guys are so selfless in this department." At that moment, I knew why I helped that customer. It was neither for her nor me but it was a teaching moment for the new team member to see selflessness in action.

My point in telling this story is not to convince you, reader, that selflessness is solely about giving money but to encourage you to think about others more than you think about yourself. You will see good things happen to you and to the organization because of your acts of selflessness. I recall a doctor on our team who celebrated her birthday by giving gifts to others. She did not expect anything in return but her act of giving caused others to smile. I realized that one act of kindness can make a huge difference in another person's life. Now I ask you, can you be that selfless person when your manager is calling your name all day or when most of your customers are impatient? Remember that you have the power to change the situation. "How?" you ask. Focus all of your attention on the needs of the customer and how you can meet those needs.

One morning a group of us were on our way to do volunteer work in the community. We stopped at a restaurant for breakfast. As I placed my order, the
customer service associate was engrossed in a conversation with another associate about events in her life. As I listened to the conversation, I thought that she just needed to talk about whatever was bugging her. Ten minutes passed and no food; so, I politely asked how much longer before my order would be ready. She realized that she had taken the order but not filled it. At that point, she was scrambling around attempting to fill the order that was placed ten minutes earlier. Clearly, her issues were more important than the customers that she was responsible for serving and her actions were a poor reflection on the company for whom she worked. My first thought was that someone needs to teach her that customer service is not about her, but it is about serving others.

Selflessness is a necessary part of excellent customer service; therefore, I encourage you to work on creating a selfless attitude and practice it.

Mind Your Own Business

Another nugget of wisdom that I have learned over the years is to mind your own business. There are some questions that we just don't need to ask. Our duty is to serve each customer with excellence. Respect and kindness are key attributes of excellence. I recall walking into an office and a clerk had sprayed so much air freshener I could hardly breathe. Her statement to me about the previous customers was very unkind. Is this the kind of behavior you want your next customer to see? Allow me to answer for you: NO!

I have seen employees ask customers questions about where they work and if their company is accepting employment applications. Can these questions be considered as networking? What does the customer think? It is important that you stick with the questions that pertain to the need of the customer. Don't assume that everyone tells their business. Allow the customer to talk; you listen.

6 CONSISTENT

Have you ever walked into a business and the entire team welcomed you as you entered? Do you remember how welcome you felt and how glad you were that you chose that particular business? But...the next time you visited that same business you did not receive that same excited greeting. I'm sure there was some disappointment because you expected that welcome. What happened? Their approach to greeting their customers was inconsistent I learned how the importance of consistency one day at work. As you know by now, I am naturally energetic. No matter the state of the office, I aim to give my best to everyone that walks in or calls. One day I was the only person in the office. The waiting room was full and the phones were ringing. My focus was to meet the needs of all of the customers and remind them that they were important to our organization. There was a young woman in the group who had had a really bad. As she approached the window, she told me how observing my work and talk with the customers on the phone had changed her perspective on what she was facing. She said she watched how I worked and how I seemed to love what I was doing. She said that she asked another customer, "I wonder if she is like this each day?" The customer that she asked replied, "Yes, she is always that way each time I have come in here." Because I was consistent in my work and did not allow the busyness of the office to overwhelm me, the customer knew how much I valued her business

Remain consistent in your service to your customers. Always remember that your customers' needs must be met and you must meet them with a spirit of excellence. Set the standard for consistency and abide by it. Your customers will be appreciative.

Let's Work on It

Identify areas in your service delivery in which you can improve your consistency.

List them below and develop strategies to improve those areas.

_____
_____
_____
_____
_____
_____
_____

Reflections

I'm super excited not because this little book has come to an end but because you are on your way to becoming an *exceptional* customer service representative. As you work in the field of customer service, hone your skills and find creative ways to serve your customers with a spirit of excellence. Always allow serving others to be your primary focus and care. Be reminded that service is about helping others get what they need. When others succeed, you succeed!

At it's greatest..IMPRESSIVE CUSTOMER SERVICE

https://www.merriam-webster.com/dictionary/selflessness
definition retrieved online 2/27/2018

ABOUT THE AUTHOR

Trishuna Brown is a servant leader who strives to help people recognize their value in serving others. She believes that excellent customer service is an attribute that every person should possess. Trishuna works in tandem with her husband Chad who is a Youth Pastor at their church. She and her husband reside in Conyers, GA with their three daughters.